Alfred Seelye Roe

Richmond, Annapolis and Home

Alfred Seelye Roe

Richmond, Annapolis and Home

ISBN/EAN: 9783337292935

Printed in Europe, USA, Canada, Australia, Japan

Cover: Foto ©Thomas Meinert / pixelio.de

More available books at **www.hansebooks.com**

PERSONAL NARRATIVES

OF EVENTS IN THE

WAR OF THE REBELLION,

BEING PAPERS READ BEFORE THE

RHODE ISLAND SOLDIERS AND SAILORS

HISTORICAL SOCIETY.

FOURTH SERIES — No. 17.

PROVIDENCE:
PUBLISHED BY THE SOCIETY.
1892.

RICHMOND, ANNAPOLIS,

AND

HOME.

BY

ALFRED S. ROE,

(Late Private, Co. A, Ninth New York Heavy Artillery Volunteers.)

PROVIDENCE:
PUBLISHED BY THE SOCIETY.
1892.

Richmond, Annapolis,

and Home.

————◆————

The horrors of that night, from Danville to Richmond, can never be effaced from memory's tablet. Eighty well men in one ordinary box car would certainly be uncomfortable, but when we remember that these prisoners had suffered much from long imprisonment, that there were men in the car who could not stand alone, that the scurvy, dysentery, and many other ailments had their representatives, some notion of the night that was before us may be had. We were disposed to endure a great deal, for we knew that our way was homeward, but the con-

Note.—For preceding experiences of the author, see his papers, No. 10, Third Series, "Recollections of Monocacy;" No. 1, Fourth Series, "From Monocacy to Danville;" and No. 16, Fourth Series, "In a Rebel Prison: or, Experiences in Danville, Va."

dition at times, seemed absolutely unendurable. The air was very keen and frosty, as cold as it often gets in the latitude of southern Virginia, so in our poorly clad state, it seemed necessary to have the car door shut. The interior, in some respects, soon resembled that of the famous Black Hole of Calcutta. The guard who stood at the door suffered with the rest of us. The moment the door was shoved open for a breath of air, some freezing wretch would clamor for its immediate closing. Finally, I asked and obtained the privilege of going to the top of the car to ride there. Since there was no danger of any one's trying to escape, my proposition found favor at once, both from the guard and from my fellow prisoners who wanted my room. It will be readily surmised that my move was not a jump from the frying pan into the *fire*. On the contrary, quite the reverse. My new Hades was like that described by Dante, where the lost are infernally and eternally preserved in vast masses of never melting ice. I lay down at full length upon the car, with my head towards Richmond and my face next to the car. I didn't freeze, that is evident, but I was just about

as cold as I could be and still be able to move.
Frequent stops were the order in the South during
the war. Accordingly when the train drew up at a
station it was possible for me to climb down and in
for a change. Sleep was the last thing thought of during these hours, but the obstacles within and without
being quite too numerous to be overcome. As for
myself, I alternated nearly the whole night long,
between the interior and exterior of the car. I
have very little recollection of the places or stations
past which we went, save one, pronounced Powatan,
destined, in a few months, to have a world wide fame
through the closing scenes in the great strife to be
enacted near; but I was not a prophet and so knew
nothing of the glories of the future. To me it was
simply a place named after an Indian chief whose
name I had all my life mispronounced as Powhatan,
and whose more famous daughter, Pocahontas, had
rendered a distressed Englishman most excellent
service, once on a time. I wondered whether the
scene of the saving were not near, hence accounting
for the name. Our guard, however, had not received much culture from the schools, and so was

quite unable to shed any light upon the subject. He simply knew that we were Yanks, proverbial for curiosity, whose zeal for knowledge not even months of imprisonment could extinguish.

Morning brought the sun and Richmond. I was taking one of my reliefs on the car top when the famous city came in sight. Had I then known all the bearings of the capital of the Confederacy, my exalted outlook might have given me a view of the prison of Belle Isle, for it was plainly visible at my left. This I did not know. Then I was more intent on the sight of the James, which the events of more than two hundred years had rendered historical. The bridge itself was the one soon to be burned on the flight of the Confederate president. We halt just over the stream, and are marched, as we suppose, to Libby. From the names on the street corners I soon learned that we were on Carey street. From my outside perch it had been easy for me to get pretty near the head of the line. Our march, however, was destined to be a short one, for in a few minutes we discovered ahead of us the celebrated sign "Libby & Sons, Ship Chandlers and

Grocers." I well remember saying to my nearest comrade, "Wouldn't that sign be a drawing card at a Sanitary Fair up North?" Some weeks afterwards, I was not a little pleased at seeing the same sign advertised as the most interesting object at a fair in, I think, Philadelphia.

Our march and observations were temporarily halted in front of a very large building which, from its numerous disconsolate occupants, we concluded to be a prison of some sort. Naturally we thought the prisoners unfortunates similar to ourselves, but on our making sundry remarks, we were informed in tones unmistakably Secesh, " We ain't Yanks, wer'e Rebs." There could be no doubt about that. No man, born north of Mason and Dixon's Line, could articulate in such a thin speeched manner as that. We were in front of Castle Thunder, long the prison house of Confederate deserters and political prisoners generally. Here we are made to march out in single file, that we might be the better numbered. Of course we thought our destination to be the notorious Libby, but we were pushed right along and into a building opposite, which we soon learned was

called Pemberton, and a sorry old rookery it was,
too.　It was three stories high, an old tobacco ware-
house, deserving a history of its own, but almost
entirely lost sight of in the greater reputation of its
neighbor, Libby.　We were under precisely the
same rule as the other edifice but were under a dif-
ferent name.　As we were sure that our stay was to
be very short in Richmond, we were disposed to endure all our ills with a deal of complacency, thinking them to be of brief duration.　Our food was of
the regulation pattern, corndodger, compact and almost saltless, with as much water as we could coax
out of the dribbling faucets.　We were as hungry
as famine could make us, but of this kind of ration
our stomachs were thoroughly cloyed.　We ate but
little of it and threw the remainder on the floor,
much to the disgust of our Rebel guards who assured
us that we might have to go hungry for our wastefulness ; but we ran the risk and awaited the issue.
The debris was gathered up and thrown into the
street, where it afforded causes for unlimited quar-
relling among the colored people as long as there
was anything left.　The officer who came in each

morning to count us was either a good actor or a
perfect devil, for each time that he made his appear-
ance, he came cursing and swearing up the stairs
with a revolver in one hand and his note book in the
other. He had an escort of two or three soldiers to
see that the terrible Yankees did not eat him, I suppose. He may have been Dick Turner himself, but
I cannot say. At any rate, he filled the Turner de-
scriptive list pretty well. His morning salutation
was something like this : "Fall into line, you G—
d—d Yankee sons of b—s." It was new usage to
us, but he had the advantage of us in that he had
the energy of position. We might inwardly resent,
but we thought the best thing for us to do was to
get into place just as quickly as possible. There
was no back talk, not a word, but if looks could have
killed, he had been a dead man a dozen times. His
conduct was of a piece with that generally had in
Richmond, I am told. Our views of the city, as in
Danville, had to be taken at a proper distance from
the windows. One day we heard a tremendous
hurrahing and soon saw a large number of men filing
by our building. They seemed to be in excellent

condition and spirits. We subsequently learned that they were paroled prisoners from the north who had just come up the river. They were very enthusiastically greeted by the citizens, and they acted as though they had had enough to eat in their northern residence. The contrast with the weakened condition about us was painfully apparent. They marched off, as we did, when we were well fed at home. The appointments of Pemberton were not so convenient as those of Danville, bad as we thought the latter. The sinks were at the end of the room, and the occupants of the upper floors were at the mercy of those below, for if the water were set running there then those above could wait till it suited the convenience of their compatriots for them to be served. Of course we could go below ourselves if we liked, but we were not very well received when we went traveling. The inevitable result of our want of sufficient water was a very sad condition of sanitation.

I am able to record that I was in Libby Prison, in war times, if only for a moment. Men were called for to go over to Libby for the purpose of getting some wood. Thinking it an opportunity that I could not afford to lose, I at once volunteered, and with several others went across the street to the edifice and down behind it, where on the canal or river side, we found an entrance to the lower regions. This basement seemed to be a sort of wood-house. Of course my eyes were open for what might fill them, and I remember asking the guard if he could show me the place through which Colonel Straight and his comrades escaped? He pointed out a large opening in the wall as the excavation made by the redoubtable Indiana officer, but in the light of subsequent knowledge, I am convinced that he was imposing upon me. However I was just as happy then over my information as I would have been had it been *bona fide* truth. I didn't know the difference. How frequently is ignorance bliss!

The morning of the memorable 22d of February, 1865, was destined to bring to us more than usual significance. It was to be to us the day of liberation. I cannot recall the hour, but on this day we were ordered into line and again we bade adieu to a prison-house and filed out into Carey street. Now we turn towards the east and it looks as though

2

home were in prospect. Our progress, though, is slow and there are many waitings which we try to fill in with observations on our surroundings. The "Johnny" dialect comes in for a deal of criticism. The average Southron will beat any other mortal living in dividing monosylables. To him "Guard" is always "Gyard." "You" and "we" become "You-uus" and "We-uns." He likes authority, too, and the devoted guard was kept in a constant panic, lest he was not in the right place.

It was during our march to the landing that I was guilty of my only offence in passing bad money. A year or more before, a cousin had visited my father's home, and coming directly from a commercial college, he had some of the so-called currency used in the make-believe banking of the college. Naturally he gave me a specimen of the bills, and as naturally I laid my acquisition away in my pocket. There it had remained during all my campaigning and imprisonment till this day. As before stated, we did not eat much of the food given to us by the rebels, but we were very hungry all the same. So when on our way down, the people came about us

with food for sale, anxious to get some of the northern money, there arose in me a disposition to work
off that spurious bill so long in my possession. To
cut a long story short, it bought for me a loaf of
bread, which was speedily put where it would do
the most good. Was I justifiable? Let some one
as hungry as myself answer. Any criticism from
well fed stay-at-homes will not be accepted. When
John Brown was asked if he could find any Bible
justification in his destruction of property and life
in his Harper's Ferry raid, he is said to have replied,
" Shall we not spoil the Egyptians?" After all we
were not particularly concerned about great moral
questions in those days.

In the days before my enlistment, I had been an
eager reader and an ardent admirer of Edgar Allen
Poe. Just before me was the very stream in whose
waters he is said to have swum seven miles, and I
wondered whether his course was over the route
about to be travelled by us.

I have stopped in Richmond twice since that day
in February. The first time was in the following
May, when the Sixth Corps marched down from its

camp in Manchester, opposite, and crossed the James on a pontoon bridge placed very near the point where we took the boat on our departure from the city. My original visit was confined to the vicinity of Carey street. Then I was under rebel guidance, now I was carrying a gun and we marched by the flank with fixed bayonets making, as we ascended State street, a glittering sea of burnished steel. From walk to walk there was just one mass of glistening points. The blinds of the houses were nearly all closed, for the occupants had no eyes for such a sight as this. That one view of the array of arms behind me was something of a compensation for the rigors of my introduction to the capital of the Confederacy.

My second revisiting was in February, 1888. Then I went purposely to see what I could of the places so prominent twenty-five years before. The Pemberton of the Rebellion had disappeared by fire, and in its place was an honest blacksmith shop where diligent toilers were earning a livelihood. Only a tradition places the old building on the site. Libby is yet standing, soon however to be transported to

Chicago. "Another reason," I heard a man remark,
" why that city should suffer from another conflagra-
tion." Despite the overpowering odor of phosphate
fertilizers, I have little trouble in doing the edifice
and in tracing out the spots where misery was once
so rife. I seek out the home of Jefferson Davis during the war, now the peaceful abode of a girls'
school. The capital is entered and all its resources
explored. I go into the library and note the prom-
inence of Confederate faces and flags, and I wonder
if Virginia had any history before the war. Perhaps the fact that it was a lost cause has given to
the strife a peculiar tenderness, for certain it is that
we of the north know nothing of the intensity of
the fervor with which the average southron regards
all memories of the Rebellion. Climbing to the cu-
pola of the structure I can see the whole city spread
out before me. Just at my feet is the famous eques-
trian statue of Washington, surrounded by other
notable sons of Virginia, fortunately erected before
the war, or it would not have been constructed at
all, for now the Mother of Presidents is devoting all
her resources to commemorating the memories of

her Lees and Jacksons, men who did their best to destroy that which her Washington, Jefferson, and others labored and fought to build. On the other side of the street is the church in which Davis was —shall I say, "worshiping," when the news of the breaking of the lines was brought to him and whence he made his hurried flight. And then to Hollywood where repose so many whom the nation knows. The guide will tell you that three presidents are buried here, but naturally he can only name two, for the very good reason that Monroe and Tyler are the only ones. From their graves we pass to that portion of the cemetery devoted to the Confederate dead. As we wander among the graves or stand beside the pyramidal structure that feminine devotion has reared to Confederate valor, we will doff our hats, for we know that those who met us in open fight were brave, and that they deserve of us what is a tribute to bravery everywhere, respect. There is one more place to visit, and we cross the James and stand upon the accursed soil of Belle Isle. We can find not the slightest trace of the horrors that made this name a hiss and a by-word among all Christian people. The river, however, flows by just as muddy and just as forbidding as when it formed an effectual barrier to the famishing prisoner held upon the island. Noisy and busy iron-works occupy the eastern end of the isle, and only a barren waste is found where once was suffered unutterable agony. I wonder why Chicago doesn't buy Belle Isle! Anchored out in her lake and made over again it would form another excellent reason why the World's Fair should not go to the champion boaster of this earth, whose founder has recently been discovered in the person of old Boreas himself.

We were told that we were the first detachment to go down the river under the resumption of the general cartel of exchange; but of this I am not prepared to affirm or deny. I do know that we were a very happy lot of men and boys on our way to what we called God's country, happy though we knew that we had left behind us upon the prison floor the dead bodies of two of our comrades. They had died on the very threshold of freedom. In fancy I often see those lonely bodies stretched in death, bodies whose souls had only a day or two before rejoiced with us on the advent of certain liberty; but they were not strong enough for the journey, and the cup fell from them even when at their very lips. Another who was supported by tender hands as we went down to the boat, had not the strength to leave it, and was carried back to Richmond for rebel burial.

The boat itself is only a dim image through the intervening years. I remember that in front of the pilot house were seated Gen. Robert Oulds, well-known in the annals of prisoner exchanges as the Confederate Commissioner, and by his side were Brigadier-Generals John Hays, of New York, and A. N. Duffié, of Rhode Island, the unsuccessful gar-roter in the attempted escape from Danville. They had not the least trace of any differences of opinions, and for aught that we could see they were friends of long standing. I envied the Union officers the information that I was certain the commissioner was giving them. I knew that we were passing historic scenes, but my comrades were as ignorant as myself, and the rebel guards were as stupid as usual, and that means that their education did not begin very

early. The boat picked its way very gingerly all
the distance down, for the river was well planted
with torpedoes, and the rebs knew how thoroughly
loaded they were. Some points we recognized without any informants, as a frowning fortification on
our right we readily named Fort Darling, long a
source of Federal anxiety. The Dutch Gap canal,
the scene of General Butler's efforts, is also found ;
but in the main the descent of the stream is rather
tame. At Richmond some of the men had received
long delayed boxes, and now on their way down the
river they regaled themselves with the contents.
They were objects of almost wolfish regard to their
fellow prisoners, in whose stomachs there were
vacua of long existence. How quickly we forget
our ills. An officer, whose stomach had become
pretty well filled by the contents of his box, was
about to throw overboard a cheese rind. I had been
watching the man for some time, wondering where
my share was to come in. Disgusted at such wicked
wastefulness I eagerly sought the morsel for myself.
It was given to me, but with much the same ex-
pression that a rebel officer's face wore when he saw

a half famished prisoner in Danville gnawing ravenously at an old bone that he had picked up somewhere. I believe the rebel called upon the Saviour of mankind in no reverent manner to witness that he had never seen anything so disgusting before. My donor had forgotten his own feelings a few hours previously when he too would have eaten anything that he could find, clean or filthy.

Just a little ways below Butler's canal, in fact scarcely more than around the bend, we are delighted at the sight of a man standing on the shore holding a white flag. It is Colonel Mulford, the Federal Commissioner of Exchange, and he is awaiting us. We are all excitement and naturally so. A few paces back of him are several soldiers, a sort of escort. Our boat rounds up to the landing, which we learn is Aiken's, very appropriately named, we thought, for it was just the place we had been aching to reach for many a long and weary day. The guards have difficulty in keeping us away from the side of the vessel, so anxious are we to be the first off the boat and so the first out of the Confederacy. Force only prevented many jumping from the boat

in our insane eagerness to touch the shore. Colonel
Mulford is hailed with as loud a cheer as we are ca-
pable of giving, and soon the plank is run out for us
to debark. The survival of the fittest is in order,
and those who are best preserved come to the front.
Instead, however, of our getting off in the hit-or-
miss order, characteristic of a Sunday-school pic-
nic, we are obliged to get in line that we may be
counted for the last time in the Confederacy. For
months I had been only a numeral. Every day
somebody had counted me, and I would have been
missed as one less if I had disappeared, but in no
other way. No enemy had taken my name nor ap-
parently cared for it. Now I was about to recover
my identity, to be something more than a mathe-
matical fact. I leave the vessel the eighteenth man,
and Brutus like I could have embraced the earth
upon which I trod. With one accord we try to do
justice to our liberation by vociferous shouting, but
here too we fail. Though we had used our voices
during our imprisonment, it was in no boisterous
manner, and we were quite unequal to the occasion.
Instead of the bold, manly tones of old, we found

our voices dwindled to childish trebles and our utterances scarcely more than chicken peeps.

Near by are ambulances for the conveyance of those who cannot walk, and they are many. Can I walk? Yes, to Washington, if necessary, if it only be northward, but I have overrated my strength. The sight of friendly faces and the breath of freedom have intoxicated me, and I am not conscious of my own weakness. Three miles intervene between us and the vessel that is to take us homeward. We set our faces with much determination towards Varina where we are to be received. Weariness is an absurdity. But dame nature tolerates no nonsense. She is not enthusiastic. Legs that have had no other sustenance than that afforded by scanty rations of corn-dodger for long months soon weaken. We effervesce quickly, and the distance at first so insignificant grows to a long and tedious march. Many could not make it and had to be picked up by the ambulances. However the end comes at last, and as we rise a little hillock and see the reception provided for us, tears start from many an eye. It is the 22d of February, Washington's birthday, and

all the bunting that the military and shipping possessed was flung to the breezes. What a sight for
flag-hungry eyes! To my mind there is nothing
lacking in the way of beauty in the American flag.
Poets and orators have descanted upon its glories,
but they have never done it justice, simply because
it is impossible. There are thoughts in the soul too
sublime for utterance, and such I think must be
those of a man whom necessity has separated from
his country for a time, and to whose view comes
suddenly the emblem of all that the patriot holds
dear, that for which he would offer up his life if
necessary. To add to the pleasures of the hour a
mounted band, said to be from Massachusetts, was
playing national airs. It was a greeting long to be
remembered. Red, white and blue in color har-
monized perfectly with the same in sound. The
Star Spangled Banner from brazen throats was
wafted back by gaudy pennons whose brilliant hues
flashed from every mast, and rainbow-like encircled
ship and cordage.

"Man shall not live by bread alone" was uttered
long ago, and its truth is not disputed. Equally

3

true is its converse that man cannot live on senti-
ment. For us, those vessels contained good honest
food and we knew it, and we stood not on the order
of our going as we approached them. We were a
hard looking lot. Ragged beyond description, and
as filthy as ragged. Long contact with the floors of
our prison houses had not kept our garments over
nice. Hunger was evident in every look and move-
ment. It was no trifling task to feed such a herd.
Now that we were so near something to eat, it
seemed as if we must famish before food could be
furnished to us. A waiter at the tables of the officers goes through our midst with a pail of refuse,
intending to throw it overboard. He is at once set
upon by hungry men who would rob the pail of its
contents, to such an insane pitch has their hunger
risen. It is only by main force that he breaks
through the crowd and throws away the filth, saluted
however, by a perfect howl of rage from the disap-
pointed prisoners, who manifest a disposition to
throw him over along with the garbage.

" Fall in for rations," is the most welcome remark
that we have heard in many a day, and it needs no

repetition for we are there immediately. Four hard
tack each, a small piece of boiled salt pork and a
quart of coffee were the items given us, it being
presumed that in our enfeebled condition a greater
quantity would be harmful; but I had gauged my
stomach differently, and I was certain that small
amount would not do for me. It was an easy matter to receive my portion in one place and then
slipping around to another point get a second share.
I doubled the rations of hard bread and pork, and
after stowing all this away where it was safe, I
wrapped an old bed cover that I had found about me
and sought my couch for the night, said couch being
the deck of the vessel. Were my dreams pleasant?
No follower of the advice in Thanatopsis ever laid
himself down to happier sleep.

Our ship was the *George Leary*, and when I went
to sleep she was quietly flying her colors at her dock
called Varina. When I awoke she was well on her
way to Annapolis. There was little to vary the mo-
notony of eating and sleeping till we reached Annapolis, which was on the morning of February 24th.

We leave our floating quarters and file through

the grounds of the United States Naval School, and
are soon drawn up before the headquarters in College Green Barracks. This depot was thus named
from its occupying the back premises of St. John's
College, an Episcopal institution, whose most famous graduate, I was repeatedly told while in Annapolis, was Reverdy Johnson, for many years a
distinguished member of the United States Senate
from Maryland. There was a curious company of
paroled men standing by to greet us. Much to my
surprise some one from the throng called out, "Is
that you, Roe?" I had to confess that it was Roe,
or what was left of him. My saluter was one
Schiffer, a member of the Fifth New York Cavalry,
and a fellow worker of mine in the disbursing office
at Auburn, N. Y. After handshakes and mutual in-
quiries as to how we got there, he asks me if I am
hungry. To this I have only to tell him to look at
me. It is enough. He disappears only to reappear
with a whole loaf of bread, a huge piece of boiled
beef, and two big cucumber pickles. To divide my
prizes with my nearest neighbor, Ed. Cady, is the
work of a moment. Another moment suffices to

get rid of the food, at any rate of all external indi-
cations. Schiffer continues his kind offices by asking me if I wouldn't like some money. To this
proposition I am nothing loth, and a couple of dollars are speedily transferred from him to me. Before breaking ranks we are furnished with certain
necessary utensils and told when and where to get
our rations; but I was too hungry to wait for any
cook-house signal, so as quickly as possible I made
my way to the sutler's and invested in about a foot
of Bologna sausage and a dozen ginger cookies.
With these I proceeded to the quarters assigned me
and there endeavored again to satisfy my hunger.
I had not more than eaten this last supply when the
bugle summoned us to the cook-house for food. I
took my quart cup for coffee and another for bean
soup. My cups were filled, whatever my own condition was. It was not till I had done justice to
this last installment that I began to be at all satis-
fied. I may as well state right here that hunger to
the recently paroled prisoner was like the thirst
ascribed to the drunkard, absolutely insatiable. To
paraphrase the words of the hymn, we ate but ever-

more were hungry. Many a man lost his life through indiscretion in eating. I must think that I owed my own life to the fact that my stomach was tolerably new, and so far as I was concerned, had been pretty well used, *i. e.*, I had never abused it by excesses of any sort. The middle-aged men and those who had been hard drinkers found the new ordeal a very severe one. As I regard the matter now, I wonder what I did with so much food, but it was no wonder to me then. The fifty-seven dollars of half ration money paid to me at the barracks was nearly all expended in what I called getting even with time. If this was money for food that I had not eaten, then I clearly owed it to myself to eat its value as soon as possible. It was not till months afterward that the unnatural craving for food wore off. To anticipate a little, when I reached home my appetite was at high water mark, and I became the great wonder of the neighborhood. I could not wait for breakfast before beginning to eat; a luncheon in the forenoon was always necessary; my dinner was a hearty one, and there had to be a filling in time long before supper, and after that, usually final meal, I found it desirable to take a parting mouthful before retiring. Chinking, so to speak, was had constantly in the way of pop-corn and apples. I lived through it; many didn't.

After we had had time to attend to the demands of hunger, our very careful supervisors ordered us to the bath-house, where we were stripped of every rag of apparel and subjected to a most thorough scrubbing with hot water and soap. The cast-off clothing was piled up like a small hill outside of the building. In my haste and happiness to get rid of my old prison reminders, I failed to take from my pocket the remainder of the money that my comrade, Schiffer, had loaned me. When my loss occurred to me it was too late to remedy it, for a long and diligent search among the filthy cast-off rags availed me nothing. In a pile of several thousand United States garments he would be a wise man who could recognize his own breeches.

At the instigation of Schiffer, I remained a few days at the College barracks to assist, but I found that my long lack of familiarity with the pen had served to make me almost a child again, so I was of little

use in the office. I was too weak for the room where
clothing was dealt out. Besides, I knew that away
up north a family was wondering where the oldest
boy was, and the tugs at my heart strings were
stronger than I could resist. I might linger here to
tell of the fun that those who were regularly de-
tached had at their quarters; of the quaint and
queer tricks they played; of the surroundings of
the barracks; but these items would not have sufficient bearing on my story. I managed to see
something of the city, famous in our national annals.
I sat in the very room where Washington stood
when he resigned his commission as commander of
the Revolutionary armies, and I crawled to the very
top of the state house. I actually went up on hands
and knees, because my legs failed me in the stair-
climbing business.

Concluding that my duty called me home at the
earliest moment possible, I asked for a transferral to
parole camp. This was located some three or four
miles west of the city and had accommodations for
several thousand men. Eating and talking over
late hardships, along with the comparing of notes

with men from other prisons, formed our chief occupation here. My furlough and my departure come speedily and happily, I make my way to Baltimore, and thence by the Northern Central Railroad I journey homeward. The only incident of this trip worthy of mention, is the stopping for dinner in Williamsport, Penn. There was a great throng at the restaurant, and before I could get to the table the bell rang for us to go aboard the cars. What was I to do? I had paid my dollar and-a-half— dinners cost something in those days—and had not had a mouthful. My old haversack was at my side. It would hold everything but coffee. I resolved to put it to the test. Accordingly I made my way to the table, regardless of ceremony, and procured a cup of coffee which I drank at once. Then, opening the wide mouth of my haversack, I tumbled in everything that I could reach. Bread, meat of all descriptions, vegetables as I could find them, till the well-filled interior of the bag reminded me that I must have my money's worth. This was not done on the sly, I'll assure you, for I was the observed of all observers, receiving from them hearty cheers while I was filling up. The supply was ample for me even, clear up to my reaching home. It was on this trip that a fellow passenger indulged in the profanity alluded to in a former paper, over a piece of my ration preserved from Danville.

Reaching Elmira late at night, and having to leave early in the morning, I enter a saloon and solicit the privilege of spreading my blanket on the floor for a few hours, a favor readily granted. This is no hardship for me, since I am used to a bed on the floor. The unceasing din of noisy drinkers does not disturb me in the least. At the proper hour I took the train for Watkins, and went by boat to Geneva on the old New York Central Railroad. As I wandered over the boat I was not a little pleased to find it the very one in which I had journeyed southward a year before. I knew it, for written on the smoke stack was my own name, placed there, boy-like, by myself. I felt as if I had found an old friend.

The great throbbing engine cannot bear me swiftly enough, now that I am on my homeward way. Eastward we fly, through Syracuse, Rome, Utica, till finally I am deposited in Herkimer, whence I am to make my trip by foot to Middleville, six miles further north. My entire way is along the banks of the West Canada Creek, whose waters some miles above form the famous Trenton Falls, but I am not just now æsthetically inclined. I am going home as fast as my strength will admit. Of course I should have gone to a stable and hired a conveyance, but again I overrated my powers of endurance. I had walked this same road repeatedly before, and why not now! I had progressed only a little way when it became painfully apparent that I could not hold out. Accordingly I called at the next house and asked the farmer if I could hire him to carry me to Middleville. This he consented to do for a dollar and-a-half. Snugly ensconced in a sleigh with plenty of buffalo robes about me, I made the remainder of the journey comfortably.

Reaching the village, I dismiss my driver as soon as I arrive in sight of the lighted windows in the parsonage. It is more than a year since I saw the interior of that house, and eight months since I have heard from any of its occupants. What changes may not have taken place in that interval! Is it any wonder that I do not wish any outsider to witness the meeting? The curtains are down, so I get no revelation as I approach. Drawing the cape of my overcoat above my head I advance to the door and knock. Soon a step approaches. I think it that of my father. The door opens and father stands before me. The soldier coat for a moment confuses him, but it is for a moment only, for he speedily exclaims, " Why, my son," and grasps me warmly by the hand. By this time I have entered the room where mother takes me to her heart as only a mother can. My sister disputes with her the possession of my head and shoulders, a seven years old brother is hugging for dear life the lower part of my body; but through all this I am sensible there is something lacking. My anxious look is detected. My eyes have indicated what my tongue dare not utter. My brother, just in his teens, is missing. Mother, whose hair has silvered rapidly during my absence, says, " You are looking for Mort." This was and is the home name of Mortimer, the playmate of my boyhood. " He is not at home now. He has se-

cured a place to work in Auburn." What a sigh of
relief I drew, for I feared that the vacancy indicated that the boy at home had succumbed to that
which his soldier brother had escaped. A telegram
speedily summons him, and ere many hours the
family is reunited. Of the comparing of notes, of
the battles fought over, of the rejoicings that home
was found, why take your time to tell? They are
in the lives and experiences of every listener who
went to the war and then came back to his home
again.

Perhaps, however, I shall never have a better opportunity to say a word about those who saw the
home side of the war. We who went down to the
strife, carried the guns, and as we thought then, en-
dured all the hardships, knew nothing of the terrible anxiety of those whom we left behind us. The
great majority of the rank and file were irresponsi-
ble boys who were fairly happy when their stomachs
were full and the marches were not too long. Of
what a father's sensations might be I had not the
slightest notion till long after the din was over.
The older men of our comrades did not receive from

4

us the consideration that I now think was their due. They were frequently laughed at as blue and gloomy when all of us would have been just the same had we had equal responsibilities. But young and old we had the consolation of action. The march, the bivouac, the fight, all these served to distract the mind and prevent its dwelling on thoughts which brought heaviness. Not so in the home. There a never wanting sense of loneliness abode. The one absent in body was ever present in mind. The danger to which he was exposed was, if possible, magnified till the anxious soul fairly consumed itself in its ceaseless vigils. Every report of new movements at the seat of war, brought with it the wonder whether the dear one would be endangered, and of these contemplated movements those at home knew vastly more than did we ourselves, who were actors in the drama. How the papers were read! The popular newspaper era in this country may be said to date from the days of the war, when the correspondent learned what the people wanted for news. Was there a battle! With what feverish haste the paper was devoured, dreading, fearing,

lest the name dearest of all may appear among the
fatalities.

A father enters the home with a copy of the *New
York Herald* in his trembling hand. The wife and
mother who had watched for his return knows that
he brings sad news. The corps to which their boy
belongs they know has been designated for a peril-
ous task, and this paper tells the story of the fight
and of the casualties. The father cannot trust himself to speak, but he points to one name among the
missing, and then betakes himself to his closet for
prayer, his refuge in every hour of distress. The
mother reads the name of her first born, as not ac-
counted for, and what boots all the rest? Patriot
though she is to her heart's core, she cannot help the
question, "Is the purchase worth the price?" With
what diligence must she pursue her household du-
ties to prevent the weight of her calamity crushing
her. Anon, she searches for the father, and finds
him with his Bible in hand looking for comforting
passages. His hands tremble as he turns the leaves
of the well-read book, and here and there he finds
words that to him afford comfort. He has preached

from these to many a congregation when their dead
were brought home to them, and now he must face
the dread possibility. Will his faith shrink? I
think not. Through those eyes a long line of pat-
riotic ancestry is looking, and though the sacrifice
were thrice as great there would be no faltering with
him. But such tests bring their inevitable results
in premature age. Many a boy left his parents
with not a token of advancing years visible in them,
and after a few months' absence returned to find
wrinkles and gray hairs making sad inroads on his
parents' faces. During the furlough, following my
imprisonment, it was my pleasure to sit at the table
of certain aged relatives who had for sundry reasons
always possessed an unusual regard for me. Said
the gentleman, " We have never sat at this board,
during all the months of your being with the Rebels,
without wishing you might have some of the food
before us ; and we have never knelt at the family
altar without bearing you in our prayers to the
throne of the Heavenly Grace." Behind the most of
us, who imperiled health and life, there were just
such prayers constantly ascending and whatever our

own lives, we were not sorry that this praying con-
tingent was ceaseless in its activity.

Our battling was that home in the broadest and
deepest sense might exist in all this fair land; that
no nominal owner might separate the father from his
children, a wife from her husband. Our fight was
a winning one, and with the end of our fighting was
the end of the glaring and flaunting lie that one
man could hold and enslave his fellow man. Hence-
forth the flag that we had followed was to float over
a race of free men, free to come and go, free to
make and hold, what I have tried to picture here, a
Home.